Vietnam War

In

50 Events

James Weber

Copyright © 2015

All rights reserved. This book or any portion thereof may not be reproduced or used in any manner whatsoever without the express written permission of the publisher except for the use of brief quotations in a book review.

About the Author:

James Weber is an author and journalist. He has a passion for literature and loves writing about social sciences, focusing on history, economics and politics. His hobbies include rowing, hiking and any other outdoor activity. James is married and has two kids.

Other Books in the *History in 50 Events* Series

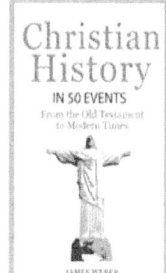

Contents

Introduction 1

From the August Revolution to the Division of Vietnam 3

    1) August 19, 1945 - The August Revolution Begins 4

    2) September 2, 1945 - Vietnam Declares Independence 5

    3) September 1945 - British Forces Arrive in Vietnam 7

    4) February 28, 1946 - Ho Chi Minh Sends Letter to President Truman 8

    5) December 19, 1946 - The First Indochina War Breaks Out 10

    6) January 18, 1950 - Soviet Union and China Recognize North Vietnam 11

    7) April 7, 1954 - Eisenhower Coins "Domino Theory" 13

    8) May 7, 1954 - French Surrender at Dien Bien Phu 14

    9) July 21, 1954 - Vietnam Is Divided 15

The Conflict Escalates: From the Mass Immigration to the Attack on Camp Holloway 19

    10) September 1954 - Mass Emigration to South Vietnam 20

    11) December 20, 1960 - National Liberation Front Formed 22

    12) May 12, 1961 - Vice President Johnson Visits South Vietnam 23

    13) February 27, 1962 - Diem Survives Assassination Attempt 24

    14) December 29, 1962 - Strategic Hamlet Program Is Called a Success 26

15) January 2, 1963 - Battle of Ap Bac 28

16) May 8, 1963 - Hue Phat Dan Shootings 29

17) June 11, 1963 - Thich Quang Duc Self-Immolates 31

18) November 2, 1963 - Ngo Dinh Diem Is Assassinated 32

19) August 2, 1964 - Gulf of Tonkin Incident 34

20) November 3, 1964 - President Johnson Is Re-elected 35

21) February 7, 1965 - Viet Cong Attack Camp Holloway 37

American Involvement: From the First US Soldiers to the Battle of Khe Sanh 39

22) March 2, 1965 - Operation Rolling Thunder 40

23) March 8, 1965 - First US Soldiers Arrive in Vietnam 41

24) March 24, 1965 - First Anti-War Teach-in 43

25) June 1965 - First Search and Destroy Missions 44

26) August 31, 1965 - Punishment for Draft-Dodging Is Increased 46

27) August 31, 1965 - US Bombing Halt 48

28) November 14, 1965 - Battle of Ia Drang 49

29) November 27, 1965 - Pentagon Advises Troop Increase 51

30) June 1966 - Operation Rolling Thunder Continues 52

31) April 15, 1967 - Martin Luther King, Jr. Demonstrates Against the War 53

32) October 21, 1967 - March on the Pentagon 55

33) January 21, 1968 - Battle of Khe Sanh 56

The Vietnam Disaster? From the Tet Offensive to the Kent State Shooting 59

34) January 31, 1968 - Tet Offensive 60

35) February 28, 1968 - Westmoreland Demands More Troops .. 61

36) March 16, 1968 - My Lai Massacre 63

37) March 31, 1968 - President Johnson Declines Re-election 64

38) May 10, 1969 - Battle of Hamburger Hill 66

39) June 1969 - Nixon Advocates Vietnamization 67

40) September 2, 1969 - Ho Chi Minh Dies 69

41) December 15, 1970 - Nixon Declares War Is Ending 70

42) April 30, 1970 - Cambodia Campaign Begins 72

43) May 4, 1970 - Kent State Shootings 73

The Last Years: From Operation Linebacker to the Fall of Saigon .. 77

44) May 9, 1972 - Operation Linebacker 78

45) January 27, 1973 - Paris Peace Accords Signed 79

46) March 29, 1973 - US Withdraws Troops from Vietnam 80

47) June 1973 - Case–Church Amendment 82

48) August 9, 1974 - President Nixon Resigns 83

49) April 9, 1975 - Battle of Xuan Loc 85

50) April 30, 1975 - The Fall of Saigon 86

Other Books in the *History in 50 Events* Series**Error! Bookmark not defined.**

Introduction

The Vietnam War dominated the country's history for the better part of the last century. What initially began as a communist revolt against French colonial power in the 1940s turned into one of the most important proxy-conflicts during the Cold War. Fighting started after World War II and did not end until 1975 with the invasion of Saigon.

What is most commonly considered the actual "Vietnam War" was the American military intervention from 1965 to 1973. US troops supported South Vietnamese soldiers against the communist forces from the North, led by their icon, Ho Chi Minh. He had defeated the French in 1954, after which peace accords were negotiated that divided the country into a communist North and a nationalist South. Even though the peace treaty included a ceasefire, North Vietnam soon broke the agreement and attacked several border regions and American military bases. Wanting to reunite the country under one single communist government, Ho Chi Minh mobilized guerilla forces in the South to destabilize the pro-American government.

Within a few years, the conflict escalated and the US government sent hundreds of thousands of American troops to help combat the communists in a war that was unlike any other before. The North Vietnamese Army (NVA) and the guerilla Viet Cong used booby traps and underground tunnels to make up for their lack of equipment and to hide from bombardment. After heavy casualties and growing protests at home, the US government eventually withdrew from Vietnam in 1973, after which the NVA invaded the

South Vietnamese capital of Saigon and succeeded in reuniting the country. Historians estimate that the conflict cost more than four million civilian lives and about 1.3 million soldiers from North and South Vietnam. Of the American soldiers, 58,200 died or went missing in action.

James Weber

From the August Revolution to the Division of Vietnam

1) August 19, 1945 - The August Revolution Begins

Many experts name the August Revolution of 1945 as the first step leading up to the Vietnam War. It was launched on August 19 by the Viet Minh (meaning "League for the Independence of Vietnam") against French colonial rule over the country. Within two weeks, they managed to seize control of many rural villages and cities throughout Vietnam. Their leader, Ho Chi Minh, would later declare independence and announce the formation of the Provisional Democratic Republic.

The revolts in Hanoi capital on August 19, 1945

Before the revolution, Vietnam had been given nominal independence by the Japanese towards the end of World War II in March 1945. The former French Governor was arrested and replaced by emperor Bao Dai. However, Bao Dai proved to care little for Vietnamese independence, and many saw him as nothing more than a Japanese puppet. After WWII and the defeat of the Japanese troops, the Allies ordered North Vietnam to be controlled by the Chinese, while South Vietnam was to surrender to British Commonwealth forces. The population saw this move as another lost chance for independence after Ho Chi Minh's earlier effort to negotiate a separation from colonial Europe had failed in 1919.

2) September 2, 1945 - Vietnam Declares Independence

Just hours after Japan surrendered to the Allied forces in World War II, communist leader Ho Chi Minh declared the independence of the new Republic of Vietnam from France. He paraphrased the American Declaration of Independence in proclaiming that from then on, "all men are born equal with inviolable rights, life, liberty, and happiness." His words were accompanied by a cheering crowd, which gathered in Hanoi's Ba Dinh Square.

The reading of the Proclamation of Independence in Hanoi

Ho Chi Minh was born in 1890 and left the country as a young cook to work on a French steamer for several years. He traveled extensively, living in London, Paris, and many other European cities. Inspired by the communist revolution in Russia, he studied revolutionary tactics in the Soviet Union and was a founding member of the French Communist Party in 1920. Later efforts to organize exiled Vietnamese communists in China got him expelled in 1927, after which he again travelled the world and only returned to Vietnam in 1941. Once there, he formed the Viet Minh, a guerrilla-fighting unit for Vietnamese independence. After the August Revolution and the surrender of Japan on September 2, 1945, he saw his chance to lead his country into a new era.

3) September 1945 - British Forces Arrive in Vietnam

As part of the Potsdam Agreement at the end of World War II, some five thousand British troops were deployed to southern Indochina to disarm the defeated Japanese army. At the same time, Ho Chi Minh and his Viet Minh guerrilla troops had seized power of the Vietnamese government. British General Douglas Gracey then ordered the rearming of more than a thousand French soldiers, who had been imprisoned by the Japanese, in order to end the revolution and reestablish French rule.

French soldiers after being freed by the British

The two sides, the French supported by the British and the Viet Minh, clashed on September 22 when the released French troops entered Saigon and attacked their opponents while killing hundreds of civilians, including children and women. They were aided by many French civilians who joined the rampage. Only two days later, the Viet Minh successfully organized a general strike to shut down all commerce, along with water supplies and electricity. Some of them would later kill more than a hundred French and Eurasian civilians in an act of retaliation for the French crimes. The unrest in Saigon also caused the first American death in Vietnam, when Officer Peter Dewey was killed by guerrillas who mistook him for a French soldier.

4) February 28, 1946 - Ho Chi Minh Sends Letter to President Truman

On February 28, 1946, Ho Chi Minh wrote a letter to US President Harry S. Truman. He used the Office of Strategic Services station in Kunming, China to ensure quick delivery to the White House. In his letter, Ho Chi Minh asked for American support in Vietnam's fight for independence from France. He hoped to negotiate a peaceful settlement with the French government once US support was promised.

The original letter sent to President Truman

Truman ignored his request, a decision some historians see as one of the biggest missed opportunities in modern history. Officially, the United States did not support the Vietnamese struggle against European colonial powers, but also ignored French pleas for help after the Viet Minh forced them to flee the country in 1954. In later years, the American government gradually increased interventions in Vietnam's civil war, which would lead to the Vietnam War. Today, Ho Chi Minh's letter is part of the National Archives.

5) December 19, 1946 - The First Indochina War Breaks Out

After negotiations between French leaders and Ho Chi Minh about a peaceful settlement of Vietnamese Independence failed, France declared the southern region of the country an official French colony. This led Minh to return to Hanoi and gather his Viet Minh troops. On December 19, 1946, he ordered around 30,000 Viet Minh soldiers to attack French positions in Hanoi.

French soldier patrolling in a communist-controlled area.

The beginning years of the war involved a guerilla insurgency against French troops in the region. However, once the Chinese communists reached the northern border of Vietnam, the fighting turned into a traditional war between both sides, equipped with modern weapons which the US and the Soviet Union supplied. French forces were made up of colonial troops from Morocco, Algeria, and Tunisia as well as trained elite soldiers and units of the French Foreign Legion. Metropolitan recruitment was forbidden by the government, as the fighting became unpopular in France. In total, the conflict lasted nine years and ended with the International Geneva Conference on July 21, 1954. Here, the new socialist French government and the Viet Minh signed an agreement that was later denounced by the government of Vietnam and the United States. It effectively gave control over North Vietnam to the communists control under leadership of Ho Chi Minh. The south was to be ruled under Emperor Bao Dai, who would be deposed a year letter by Ngo Dinh Diem, his prime minister. This created several conflicts within North Vietnam, which subsequently escalated into the Vietnam War.

6) January 18, 1950 - Soviet Union and China Recognize North Vietnam

On this day, the People's Republic of China formally recognized the Democratic Republic of Vietnam under communist leadership of Ho Chi Minh. The Soviet Union extended diplomatic recognition to Vietnam a few days later. China's wish to play a larger role in Asia, as well as its deepening suspicions of Western politics in neighboring Vietnam, pushed the government toward closer relations with Vietnam. Quickly after the official declaration of recognition, China started sending immense quantities of military assistance into

Vietnam. Both China and the Soviet Union pledged to support the new republic in its fight against France with weapons and equipment. Furthermore, a bill to supply economic aid for the young country was passed.

The official flag of the new North Vietnamese Republic

The US answered by supporting the French in Vietnam more actively. Several months after China's recognition of North Vietnam, the American government asked Congress for increased military aid, which was provided. All three countries – the US, Russia, and China – dramatically increased their roles in the Vietnamese conflict in the years to come. The Chinese aid between 1950 and 1970 to North Vietnam has been estimated at more than $20 billion. Some believe that three-quarters of the total military support since 1949 came from China, with the Soviets providing the rest. Without the aid from its big allies, continuing the war would have been impossible for North Vietnam.

7) April 7, 1954 - Eisenhower Coins "Domino Theory"

In a speech given on April 7, 1954, President Eisenhower suggested that a fall of French Indochina to the communist regime could set off a domino effect in Southeast Asia. According to the theory, other countries would soon follow as communism spread. His theory dominated much of American thinking about Vietnam throughout the next decade. In 1954, it had become clear that French troops were failing in their mission to regain control over the country and establish colonial control again. In the battle of Dien Bien Phu, Vietnamese nationalists defeated the French forces, which grew weaker in the entire country in the following weeks.

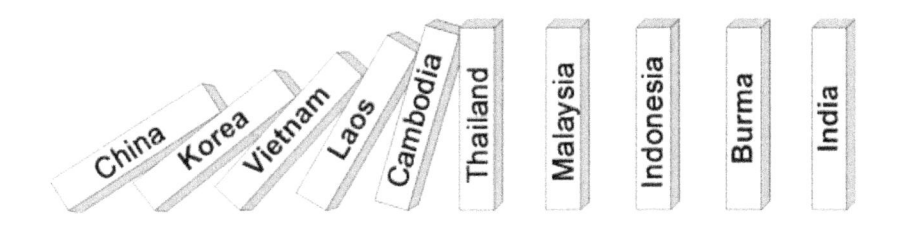

In order to gain national support for a higher degree of US aid, Eisenhower held a press conference explaining the significance of Vietnam as a country. He emphasized on a series of economic as well as moral arguments for his cause. According to Eisenhower, Vietnam's production of materials such as rubber, sulphur, and jute was invaluable to the rest of the world and could only be guaranteed under capitalism. He also condemned the new republic as a *de facto* dictatorship, disregarding many human rights. Though rhetorically well presented, Eisenhower's speech had little initial impact. The communists continued to gain territory and increased their guerilla forces in the south.

8) May 7, 1954 - French Surrender at Dien Bien Phu

After 57 days of siege, Ho Chi Minh's Viet Minh forces defeated the French troops at their stronghold in Dien Bien Phu. This decisive victory marked the end of French influence in Indochina and paved the way for a division of the country along the 17th parallel.

Viet Minh raise their flag over a French position

Dien Bien Phu, a tiny mountain outpost close to Laos, became of importance for both sides after the French, tired of jungle warfare, seized control over it in November 1953. Even after the Vietnamese cut off all roads to the fort, French soldiers remained confident that air supply meant they still had the upper hand. The open position of Dien Bien Phu also allowed them to use artillery against far away targets. In early 1954, General Vo Nguyen Giap decided to invade the fort with his Viet Minh army, encircling the French only a few days later with 40,000 soldiers and heavy weaponry. On March 12, the communists launched their first attack against the entrenched French troops, who had a hard time defending their positions. Air support could not supply the necessary back up and ammunition to successfully fight off the enemy. On May 7, their positions collapsed and all French troops surrendered.

9) July 21, 1954 - Vietnam Is Divided

After the French surrender which marked the end of the First Indochina War, a peace conference was held in Geneva, Switzerland, in July 1954 to decide on the future of the Southeast Asian continent. Several countries sent representatives, such as the United States, the Soviet Union, France, the United Kingdom, as well as the People's Republic of China. During the conference, Pierre Mendes-France, the newly appointed French Prime Minister, signed an agreement with representatives from Vietnam that would end the war that had cost more than 300,000 lives. Even though the peace accord caused relief in Europe, especially in France, it greatly concerned US President Eisenhower. Part of the main agreements of the Geneva Accord were:

- A division of Vietnam along the 17th parallel, resulting in two separate countries.

- The North would become a communist state led by the Viet Minh leader Ho Chi Minh and the South a nationalist state with Emperor Bao Dai and Prime Minister Ngo Dinh Diem.
- The respective capitals were to be Saigon in the south and Hanoi in the north.
- Elections had to be held in 1956 with the goal of a unified government.
- All prisoners of war had to be released, while French forces would withdraw from the north.

Though Eisenhower did not sign the agreement, as he feared that a separation of the country would cause further conflict, he promised military aid to the South. Many historians believed that the accords were forced on the French, who sought a quick fix after their surrender. Therefore, the outcome of the conference can be seen as a victory for the communists.

James Weber

The Conflict Escalates: From the Mass Immigration to the Attack on Camp Holloway

10) September 1954 - Mass Emigration to South Vietnam

After Dien Bien Phu fell to the communists and the country had been officially divided, the United States decided to transport more than 300,000 Vietnamese civilians and non-Vietnamese members of the French Army into South Vietnam, as part of an operation that was called "Passage to Freedom." Since the Geneva Accords allowed for a 300-day period of grace, in which people could freely travel between the two countries, all parties involved in the operation had less than a year for its execution. After that, the border would be sealed and no civilian would be allowed to pass. Initially, the separation of the country was to be only temporary and to be reunified in 1956.

Refugees leaving North Vietnam by sea

In total, more than half a million people moved south, and around thirty thousand civilians and some 100,000 soldiers went in the opposite direction. This mass emigration was made possible with the help of the French Air Force and Navy, supported by American ships and equipment. Most northerners were evacuated to Saigon, where they would be received by humanitarian organizations and stationed in refugee camps. The American government used news coverage of the migration as propaganda against the communist north, displaying civilians fleeing from the oppression in their homeland.

11) December 20, 1960 - National Liberation Front Formed

With the exact location unknown, North Vietnam announced the formation of the National Front for a Liberation of the South (NLF) on December 20, 1960, somewhere close to Hanoi. The conference at which the NFL was announced, hosted a series of political parties from all kinds of political backgrounds. The new army was meant to imitate the Viet Minh in its success to liberate Vietnam from colonial rule. This time, however, the objective was to unify the divided country under one communist government. It reached out to those Southerners dissatisfied with their President Ngo Dinh Diem.

A Viet Cong soldiers hiding in an underground cave

From its beginning, the military forces were seen as North Vietnam's shadow government in the South. Soon, Ngo Dinh Diem's staff called it the Viet Cong, a name that would later also be used by American media. Calm during the first years of existence, the NLF attacked US Army installations at Pleiku and Qui Nhon in 1965, leading to the deployment of thousands of US soldiers to Vietnam in March that year. Three years later, the Viet Cong reached the height of its power in the Tet Offensive against key urban centers in South Vietnam. Many of their tactics included guerilla warfare and the use of deadly booby traps.

12) May 12, 1961 - Vice President Johnson Visits South Vietnam

In May 1961, Vice President Lyndon B. Johnson visited Vietnam as part of a tour through Asia. In his three-day visit, Johnson met with South Vietnamese President Ngo Dinh Diem in the capital Saigon to discuss Vietnam's future and American involvement in the conflict with the North. President Kennedy had instructed Johnson to deliver a message stating that the US had great faith in Diem's abilities and approved an increase in South Vietnamese military forces to 170,000 (after World War II, the allowed number of Vietnamese soldiers had been limited by the Allies to around 150,000). Kennedy also offered increased military aid, which he said would not be conditioned to any social and economic reforms under the Diem government. President Ngo Dinh Diem thankfully declined the offer, believing that it showed weakness and would mean a propaganda victory for North Vietnam.

Johnson visiting American soldiers in Vietnam

On his return to the US, Johnson called Diem the "Churchill of Asia" and the only realistic alternative to communist control. He then went on to support Eisenhower's domino theory, stating that a loss in Vietnam would soon lead to fights "on the beaches of Waikiki" and later on "our own shores." After Johnson became president in 1963, he deployed more than 500,000 US troops to Vietnam.

13) February 27, 1962 - Diem Survives Assassination Attempt

On February 27, 1962, two dissident pilots of the Vietnam Air Force, First Lieutenant Pham Phu Quoc and Second Lieutenant Nguyen Van Cu bombed the Vietnamese Independence Palace. The Palace was the official residence of high officials in South Vietnam, while the bombing was meant as an assassination attempt on President Ngo Dinh Diem and his relatives, who were also his political advisors. The two Lieutenants later stated that they acted in response to Diem's oppressive rule, in which his only goal was to remain in power rather than confronting the Vietcong, who threatened to overthrow their South Vietnamese government. Quoc and Cu hoped that such an airstrike would show Diem's vulnerability and lead to a general uprising, but this failed to materialize.

An A-1 Skyraider, a similar aircraft to the one used in the attack

One of the bombs hit a room in the western wing where Diem was sleeping, though it did not detonate, leading him to believe that he possessed "divine" protection. Interestingly, Madame Nhu, Diem's sister-in-law, was the only family member to suffer minor injuries. In total, three members of the palace staff died, while thirty others were injured. Quoc was later arrested and imprisoned, but Cu managed to escape to Cambodia. Following the attack, Diem became hostile towards the US presence in South Vietnam, claiming that the foreign media was trying to bring him down. He therefore introduced several restrictions on political association and press freedom.

14) December 29, 1962 - Strategic Hamlet Program Is Called a Success

The Hamlet Program was a strategy implemented by South Vietnam with the support of the United States to fight the communist insurgency by means of population transfer during the Vietnam War. In 1961, the Diem regime, along with US advisors in South Vietnam, started the implementation of a plan to isolate rural peasants from the sphere of influence of the Viet Minh. Part of the Strategic Hamlet Program and an earlier program called the Rural Community Development Program was to create new communities of "secure hamlets." Rural peasants were to be physically isolated from the enemy's insurgents and their support services, which would indirectly strengthen ties with the South Vietnamese government. Officials hoped that this would lead to increased loyalty by the rural population towards the government. Even though the program was called a success by Diem in 1962, in the end, it led to a decrease in support for his regime and an increase in sympathy for the communist cause.

Example of a Hamlet built by the South Vietnamese government

Following the overthrow of Ngo Dinh Diem in November 1963, the program was decreasingly enforced and many moved back into their native areas. At the same time, American military advisor John Paul Vann started criticized the program in his official reports, and concerns were expressed by reporters who began to investigate more closely. Some coverages, like the one from David Halberstam on the Hamlet Program's shortcomings, gained nationwide attention. He reported that only 20% of the 8600 hamlets that the Diem regime installed met the minimum standards of readiness and security. The program officially ended in a year later. Later counterinsurgency programs tried to focus on accessing the people in their existing communities rather than through obligated relocation.

15) January 2, 1963 - Battle of Ap Bac

The Battle of Ap Bac was the first major battle of the war, and took place on January 2, 1963, in Dịnh Tuong Province, South Vietnam. Leading up to the battle, US intelligence detected a radio transmitter as well as around 120 soldiers of the National Front for the Liberation in the hamlet of Ap Tan Thoi. The hamlet was home to the 7th Infantry Division of the Army of the Republic of South Vietnam. In order to fight off the NLF soldiers, the South Vietnamese and their American advisers would attack Ap Tan Thoi from three different directions. They planned to use two provincial Civil Guard battalions and parts of the 11th Infantry Regiment. The infantry battalions would be supported by helicopters, artillery and M-113 armored personnel carriers.

Two of the five American helicopters that were shot down

In the morning hours of January 2, 1963, the South Vietnamese then marched toward Ap Tan Thoi in order to attack their enemy. However, once they reached the hamlet of Ap Bac, their advance was immediately brought to a halt by soldiers of the Viet Cong 261st

Battalion. The NLF troops had entrenched themselves and welcomed the South Vietnamese with heavy fire. In order to break open the defense, it was then decided to fly in further reinforcements with the help of American helicopters. Unfortunately, the NLF soldiers managed to shoot down five helicopters and stop several others from landing. The attack had turned into a disaster for the South Vietnamese troops, who were pinned down by their enemy and not able to retreat. Only when the Viet Cong withdrew from their positions under the cover of darkness could the South Vietnamese gather again, having suffered their first major loss.

16) May 8, 1963 - Hue Phat Dan Shootings

On May 8, 1963, Vietnamese army and police shot their guns and launched grenades into a crowd of Buddhists who had been protesting against a nationwide ban on the raising of the Buddhist flag on the day of Phat Dan, which celebrates the birth of Gautama Buddha. The Hue Phat Dan shootings resulted in the deaths of nine unarmed Buddhist civilians. President Diem later denied allegations of governmental responsibility for the incident and blamed the Viet Cong.

A monument to the Huế Phật Đản shootings

In a press conference, he stated that Viet Cong guerrilla were behind the incident and had set off the explosions, trying to undermine his authority. Diem also refused to take any disciplinary measures against the involved authorities, declaring that they had acted within their jurisdiction. Government investigations of the shooting later stated that only percussion grenades were used in the shooting and no lethal grenades. However, due to the force of the explosions, doubts were raised on whether the Viet Cong had access to such powerful explosives. A different theory at the time was that the CIA initiated the blasts trying to foment internal tensions and destabilizing the South Vietnamese regime. Witnesses disputed the government's version of events, using amateur footage that showed soldiers firing into the crowd as proof. One local doctor believed that fatal injuries could not have been inflicted by plastic explosives, a statement for which he went to jail. Diem did not change his initial statement about the incident and forbade autopsy for the bodies of the victims.

17) June 11, 1963 - Thich Quang Duc Self-Immolates

On June 11, 1963, the Vietnamese Mahayana Buddhist Thich Quang Duc burned himself to death at one of Saigon's busiest road intersections. He was protesting the discrimination of Buddhists by the South Vietnamese government under leadership of Ngo Dinh Diem. News and pictures of his self-immolation quickly spread around the globe, causing outrage while bringing attention to the policies of the Diem government and increasing international pressure for changes. Diem subsequently announced reforms with the intention of mollifying the Buddhists. Nevertheless, the promised reforms were not implemented, which led to a deterioration in the dispute. As the protests continued, the ARVN Special Forces loyal to Diem's brother, Ngo Dinh Nhu, began nationwide raids on Buddhist pagodas, taking Quang Duc's heart, while killing dozens and causing widespread damage. After the self-immolation, a series of Buddhist monks followed Quang Duc's act and also immolated themselves.

Leading up to the event, US journalists were informed on June 10 that "something important" would happen the next day on the road outside the Cambodian embassy. Many reporters dismissed the message as unimportant, as the Buddhist crisis had been going on for several weeks at that point. On June 11, only a small group of journalists showed up, including Malcolm Browne, the Saigon bureau chief for the Associated Press, and David Halberstam of The New York Times. Some time later, around 350 nuns and monks marched by in two lines with banners printed in both Vietnamese and English. They demanded that the Vietnamese government act on its promises of religious equality. The act then occurred a few streets southwest of the Presidential Palace. Duc, along with two other Buddhists, emerged from a vehicle, and one placed a pillow on the road. Another then opened the trunk and reached for a petrol can. While the marchers created a circle around Duc, he sat down on the cushion calmly. His colleague then emptied the petrol over Duc's head as Duc recited a Buddhist prayer before lighting a match and dropping it on his own body. Malcolm Browne, who took a picture of the monk, won the Pulitzer Prize for his photograph.

18) November 2, 1963 - Ngo Dinh Diem Is Assassinated

Starting on November 1, 1963, President Ngo Dinh Diem was deposed by a group of Vietnam army officers who acted on their disagreement with his handling of the Viet Cong threat and the Buddhist crisis. The US government had been aware of the coup planning, but officials later stated that it was US policy not to intervene. However, Lucien Conein, the CIA's connection between the American embassy and the coup planners, actively provided funds to the leaders. It is unclear from whom he received the money in the first place, and many suggest a US source since before the assassination, it had become clear that the American government saw Diem as an obstacle to the accomplishment of US missions in Southeast Asia. His de facto dictatorship only succeeded in alienating most of the South Vietnamese people and the Buddhist protest caused worldwide outrage. After the executing of Diem, the United States become more directly and heavily involved in the Vietnam War.

President Diệm

The coup was executed under leadership of General Dương Văn Minh and proceeded smoothly as many high officials were caught off-guard and resistance was little. The following day, Diem was executed along with his brother Ngo Dinh Nhu. Diem's death caused nationwide celebrations, but at the same time led to political chaos in Vietnam. To stabilize the situation, the US government then decided to intervene to stabilize the situation and fight the increasingly powerful guerrilla soldiers.

19) August 2, 1964 - Gulf of Tonkin Incident

The Gulf of Tonkin Incident and the USS Maddox Incident are actually two separate confrontations involving North Vietnam and the United States, though today they are usually summarized as one. On July 30, South Vietnamese special torpedo boats attacked the islands of Hon Me and Hon Ngu in the Tonkin Gulf and fired on island installations. A close by American destroyer, the USS *Maddox*, monitored the attack via radar. Three days later, the destroyer reported being attacked by a series of North Vietnamese Navy torpedo boats while performing a signals intelligence patrol. The *Maddox* then returned fire on the North Vietnamese fleet. In total, three North Vietnamese torpedo boats were damaged and four North Vietnamese sailors killed. There were no reports of American casualties.

Picture showing the three North Vietnamese motor torpedo boats

In the following weeks, it was claimed by the National Security Agency that the event occurred on August 4, as an entirely different sea battle. However, evidence of false radar images indicated a set up. Secretary of Defense Robert S. McNamara later stated that the August 2 USS *Maddox* attack happened, though with no Defense Department response, and the August 4 Gulf of Tonkin attack never really took place. The Gulf of Tonkin Resolution was passed by Congress after the incidents, which gave President Johnson the legal right to aid any Southeast Asian fearing communist aggression. It helped legally deploy conventional US troops to the region and signaled the start of open warfare against North Vietnam.

20) November 3, 1964 - President Johnson Is Re-elected

After succeeding the assassinated John. F. Kennedy as US President, Lyndon B. Johnson defeated Republican challenger Barry Goldwater in 1964 with one of the most tremendous landslides in election history. With 64 percent of the popular vote, he secured his second term and first full term in office. Senator Barry Goldwater of Arizona, the Republican candidate, lacked support from his own party due to his highly controversial conservative political positions. Johnson managed to portray Goldwater as a dangerous extremist and advocated several social programs to overcome racial segregation. His programs, collectively known as the Great Society, gained wide popularity, and he carried 44 of the 50 states in the elections.

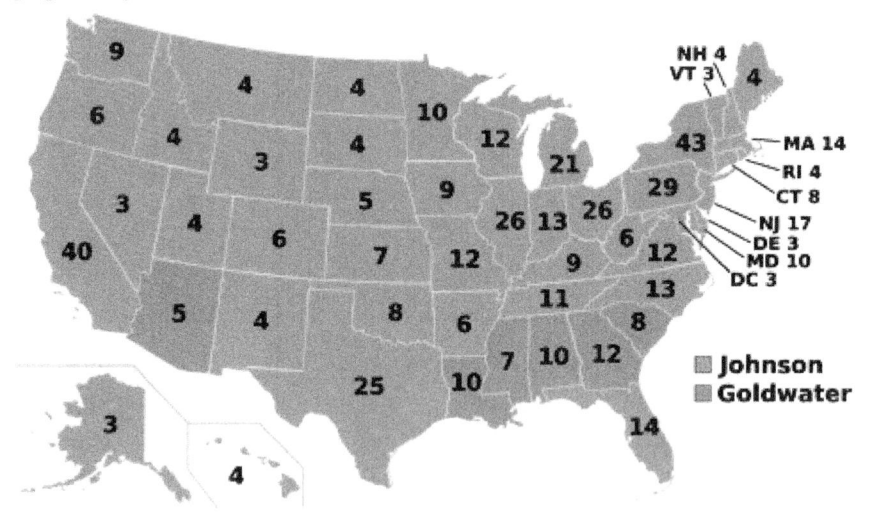

The election results map

Some of the most drastic differences between Johnson and Goldwater appeared over the question of Cold War foreign policy. Goldwater accused Johnson and his administration with having given in to communist aggression in Cuba. On several occasions, he seemed to be in favor of using nuclear weapons on both Cuba and North Vietnam. Opinions such as these made it easy for Johnson's advisors to portray Goldwater as an inhuman warmonger, with no fear to initiate World War III. Interestingly, Johnson promised the

American public not to send US troops to Vietnam in a fight that "Vietnam boys ought to be fighting for themselves." Four months after his reelection, his administration committed US combat troops to Vietnam.

21) February 7, 1965 - Viet Cong Attack Camp Holloway

During the early hours of February 7, 1965, the Viet Cong attacked the US Camp Holloway helicopter facility near Pleiku. At around 11 p.m., more than three hundred Viet Cong soldiers gathered at their positions outside Camp Holloway and began cutting through the wire fences. The ambush attack was nearly discovered when one of their combat engineers accidentally broke an electrical wire, but the US soldiers patrolling the area did not notice the broken wire. A few hours later, they opened fire on the camp with Russian AK-47 rifles and later mortared the area, destroying ten aircrafts. The entire operation lasted only a few minutes before the Viet Cong retreated. They caused the death of eight American soldiers with another 125 wounded. Just twelve hours after the attack, the US government began Operation Flaming Dart to drop bombs on selected North Vietnamese targets.

Camp Holloway before the attack

Before the attacks on Camp Holloway, the Viet Cong executed various attacks on US military facilities in South Vietnam, though President Johnson did not order retaliations against North Vietnam, trying to avoid upsetting the American public during the 1964 election campaign. The Soviets, on the other hand, experienced drastic political changes after Nikita Khrushchev was removed from office. Declining military aid during his time was reinstated and Russia's influence in Southeast Asia increased.

American Involvement: From the First US Soldiers to the Battle of Khe Sanh

22) March 2, 1965 - Operation Rolling Thunder

Following the attack on Camp Holloway, President Johnson ordered a massive bombardment by the US Air Force and Navy against the Democratic Republic of Vietnam. Beginning on March 2, 1965, and lasting until November 2, 1968, it was meant to put military pressure on North Vietnam's army and communist leaders. In total, more bombs were dropped on Vietnam than throughout World War II, intending to reduce the NVA's ability to wage war against the South. Operation Rolling Thunder was the first sustained American assault in North Vietnamese territory and marked one of the major expansions of US involvement in the Vietnam War.

A radar bombing executed by F-105 Thunderchiefs

Beside the objectives mentioned above, the operation's aim was to discourage North Vietnamese soldiers and destroy North Vietnam's logistics and industrial bases. The operation would later turn into the most intense air battle during the Cold War; some historians even call it the most difficult US Air Force campaign since the bombing of Germany in World War II. The NVA and its guerilla fighters defended their positions with sophisticated air-to-air and ground-to-air weapons they received from their communist allies China and Russia.

23) March 8, 1965 - First US Soldiers Arrive in Vietnam

With Operation Rolling Thunder on its way, the deployment of about 3,500 combat troops to Da Nang finally signaled President Johnson's intention to become fully invested in a war in Vietnam. The soldiers of the 9th Marine Expeditionary Brigade arrived on March 8, 1965, and were met by South Vietnamese officers, US military advisors, and even a group of girls carrying signs with welcome messages on them. This sort of arrival was much to the dismay of General William Westmoreland, who along with General Nguyen Van Thieu, commander of the South Vietnamese Armed Forces, had hoped for the troops to be brought into the country without much publicity.

US troops near Da Nang in 1965.

Leading up to the arrival of the 9th Marine Expeditionary Brigade, the number of American military advisors in Vietnam had risen to more than 16,000 under President Kennedy. After his death, President Johnson declared that a battle against communism in Vietnam must be met with "determination and strength." His eventual deployment of US troops caused opposition from many sides, with China and the Soviet Union threatening to intervene. This also led to the infamous attack on the US Embassy in Moscow, when some 2,000 demonstrators, including Vietnamese and Chinese students, rallied outside the building.

24) March 24, 1965 - First Anti-War Teach-in

Following the deployment of American troops to Vietnam, around two hundred faculty members of the University of Michigan at Ann Arbor participated in an official "teach-in" by giving special anti-war seminars. Teach-ins were meant as a general educational forum on any current issues, though unlike a seminar, there would be no time limit and no specific frame of topic. They were intended to be practical, with a series of discussions and sometimes the development of an action plan.

An example of an Anti-War Teach-in

The first teach-in on March 24 was held overnight, beginning with a discussion of the Vietnam War draft and ending in the early morning with a speech by philosopher Arnold Kaufman. Many regular classes were canceled the next day, as many faculty members signed onto a one-day teaching strike to protest the Vietnam War. They gathered throughout the campus to discuss alternative ways of protesting the war, while facing strong opposition from the university president, the Michigan legislature, and the governor. On March 26, a similar teach-in at Columbia University occurred. Open to a broad audience, with lectures by experts as well as the participation of normal students, the teach-ins soon gained popularity and spread to many colleges and universities.

25) June 1965 - First Search and Destroy Missions

To counter the increasing use of guerilla tactics by the Viet Cong, American General Westmorland came up with the so-called "search and destroy" military strategy. This strategy was highly aggressive and would be implemented in June 1965. The idea was to land ground forces into enemy territory, search out the enemy forces, destroy them, and immediately withdraw afterward. The missions were made possible due to the recent invention of the helicopter, which helped the US Army land in difficult terrain and fight the Viet Cong in jungle warfare.

US soldier in a search and destroy mission to hunt down Vietcong guerrillas

The conventional strategy of "clear and hold," meaning to attack and conquer an enemy's position, proved to be useless against the North Vietnamese, who set up booby traps and used underground tunnels to hide from American soldiers. The search and destroy strategy was meant to infiltrate small hideouts and eliminate as many enemy troops as possible in a matter of minutes. The infamous "body count" was then introduced to measure the success of such a mission. Although they initially seemed to work against the Viet Cong, the search and destroy missions had various flaws. Since many soldiers were still not familiar with the strategy, there was an obvious lack of distinction between traditional clearing missions and search and destroy. Often, in the beginning of the war, operations were either too brutal, which caused outrage from the Vietnamese public, or not aggressive enough to clear enemy positions.

26) August 31, 1965 - Punishment for Draft-Dodging Is Increased

On August 31, 1965, the US Congress passed an amendment to the Selective Service Act that would criminalize the destruction of draft cards. Draft cards were small notices sent to male citizens who were required to call for service in the US military. The decision of the US Congress made it illegal to avoid a possible draft by destroying the draft card. Those committing the act would face a five-year prison sentence and possibly more than $10,000 in fines.

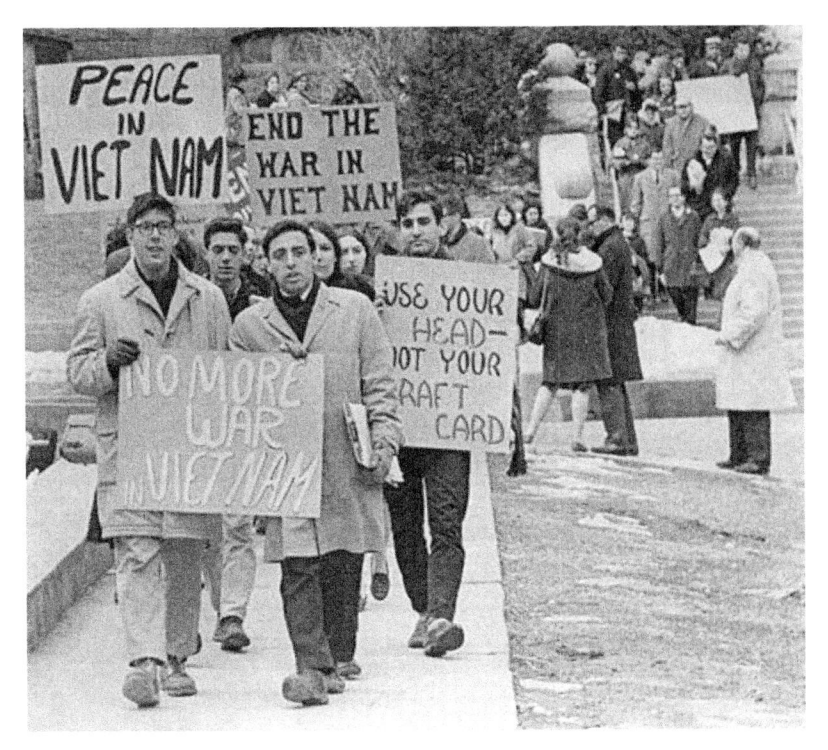

Protests against the draft increased in 1965

The amendment was initially passed as a response to increased draft evasion and draft-card burning. Both were a symbol of protest, which thousands of young American men used as part of their opposition to the Vietnam War and the involvement of the United States. Starting in May 1964, several activists burned their draft cards at demonstrations and anti-war rallies. The occurrence of such rallies increased in 1965 and soon gained nationwide attention. In order to limit such protests, the United States Congress decided to increase the punishment for draft card burning and subsequent draft evasion. After the law was passed, 46 men were prosecuted for burning their draft cards, leading to four major court cases. The case *United States v. O'Brien* reached the Supreme Court, which decided against the draft card burners and determined that the burnings did not symbolize an act of free speech.

27) August 31, 1965 - US Bombing Halt

In his attempt to spur negotiations with North Vietnam, President Johnson ordered a pause in the bombing of North Vietnam. During the following 37 days, the US attempted to pressure North Vietnam into negotiating peace under American terms. However, the negotiations failed, as North Vietnam denounced the bombing halt and was not willing to give in to the American demands. Meanwhile, the Viet Cong continued terrorist activities in South Vietnam.

During the bombing halt, raids on North Vietnam were partially or completely stopped

By the end of 1965, US troop levels in Vietnam reached almost 185,000, though a victory was not in sight. During the same time, more than 90,000 South Vietnamese soldiers deserted, while the Viet Cong and North Vietnamese guerilla soldiers infiltrated their enemy's territory via the Ho Chi Minh trail. It has been estimated that more than half of the countryside in South Vietnam was controlled by the Viet Cong.

Bombing halts to advance negotiations with North Vietnam happened several times throughout the war. In 1968, President Johnson once again announced a partial halt of bombing and offered new peace talks. However, in the same television speech, he mentioned that the US would be increasing its war expenditures to $2.6 billion and deploying another 13,500 troops to Vietnam.

28) November 14, 1965 - Battle of Ia Drang

The Battle of Ia Drang would become the first major battle between soldiers of the United States Army and North Vietnamese forces during the Vietnam War. It was a four-day battle that took place between November 14 and November 18, 1965, in the Central Highlands of South Vietnam at two landing zones west of Plei Me. The battle was part of an American airmobile offensive called Operation Silver Bayonet I. Before the landing, strategic bombing strikes had hit the region in order to weaken the NVA's defensive positions. The US troops were then able to inflict heavy losses on Viet Cong guerrillas and North Vietnamese regulars during the first days. However, on November 17, NVA overran the 2nd Battalion near a landing zone codenamed Albany and killed nearly 250 American soldiers. North Vietnamese casualties totaled around 1,000 after the battle.

American soldiers under fire after landing in enemy territory

After the battle, both sides claimed Ia Drang a victory since they had inflicted heavy casualties on their enemy. The fights are now considered essential by war historians, as they set the blueprint for strategies on both sides during the war. US troops continued to rely on the use of helicopters for air mobility and search and destroy missions, while the Viet Cong saw that they could even out American advantages by fighting at close range and overrunning their enemy.

29) November 27, 1965 - Pentagon Advises Troop Increase

Towards the end of 1965, the US involvement in Vietnam became increasingly that of an official war. On November 27, several representatives from the Pentagon sat down with President Johnson to discuss and plan troop deployment for the following year. In this meeting, President Johnson was informed that if General Westmoreland was to successfully execute the new search and destroy missions, US troops in Vietnam should be more than doubled to around 400,000 men.

Anti-War protests increased during the end of 1965

November 27, 1965 was also the date of two other important events. The Viet Cong finally released two men believed to be Special Forces soldiers, who they captured several years earlier close to Saigon during the battle of Hiep Hoa. The soldiers identified as Sgt. George Smith and Claude McClure later declared their opposition to the war and campaigned for a withdrawal of US troops. They were then put on trial for cooperating with the enemy, where Smith subsequently denied any declarations he made earlier. In the midst of their trial, some 30,000 protesters gathered at the White House and from there moved to the Washington Monument. Speeches were held by famous figures of the anti-war movement such as Dr. Benjamin Spock and Coretta Scott King.

30) June 1966 - Operation Rolling Thunder Continues

When Operation Rolling Thunder began in 1965, the US Air Force acted under clear restrictions as to which targets could be bombed. Suitable targets were transportation routes and anything of vital importance to the NVA's infrastructure. Anything in or near Hanoi and Haiphong was to be left untouched. This restriction was lifted in June 1966 when US planes struck North Vietnamese gasoline-storages in several devastating bombings. From then on, the raids were expanded to storage facilities containing ammunition, oil, or weapons. This included targets in Hanoi and Haiphong.

The use of napalm was frequent in the Vietnam War

Operation Rolling Thunder became a more controversial topic when it was further expanded the following year. Factories, power plants, and airfields could be bombed and were sometimes handpicked by President Johnson. Many Americans reacted outraged once news spread about the number of civilian casualties during the campaign. Private war reporters and journalists brought home pictures and documentaries that showed aerial-bombings taking targeted land the size of many football fields using napalm and other highly controversial weapons.

31) April 15, 1967 - Martin Luther King, Jr. Demonstrates Against the War

In 1967, an antiwar organization called the "Spring Mobilization Committee to End the War in Vietnam" formed. Informally known as the Mobe, it was made up of antiwar activists who planned large demonstrations in opposition to the ongoing war. On April 15, 1967, the Mobe organized a massive demonstration march from Central Park to the United Nations building. The march attracted hundreds of thousands of people and many famous speakers such as Dr. Martin Luther King, Jr., James Bevel, and Harry Belafonte. Even though the leaders of the march did not call for it, many protesters burned their draft cards at the march, which was supported by a simultaneous event in San Francisco.

Antiwar protestors during the March

The New York march was attended by more than 100,000 protesters from different backgrounds. Although the majority of the attendees were young students, hundreds of professors, blue-collar workers, and representatives from various religions followed the crowd. During the event, Martin Luther King, Jr., declared that the march meant a great success for the antiwar movement and would be followed by another march in Washington D.C. The planning of this event would be done during a Spring Mobilization Conference on May 20–21, 1967, with some 700 antiwar activists invited.

32) October 21, 1967 - March on the Pentagon

The second big march against the war took place on October 21, 1967. Demonstrators included radicals, professors, black nationalists, liberals, hippies, women's groups, and war veterans who marched on the Pentagon. It began in front of the Lincoln Memorial with many demonstrators waving the red, blue, and gold flags of the Viet Cong. Initially, the protests remained peaceful and were only disrupted by occasional screams and shouts. However, violence spread when a more radical part of the demonstrators encountered US Marshals protecting the Pentagon. They surrounded the building throughout the night and some even tried to storm it. At one time, 20 to 30 protesters broke through the line of US Marshals and pushed into the Pentagon's Mall entrance. They were stopped and forced outside by heavily armed troops.

Antiwar protestors during a March on the Pentagon in 1967

The next morning, by the time order was restored, 680 people had been arrested. This figure included novelist Norman Mailer as well as two United Press International reporters. Media reports later stated that similar protests took place in Japan and Western Europe. In London, outside the US Embassy, some 3,000 demonstrators almost succeeded in trying to storm the building.

33) January 21, 1968 - Battle of Khe Sanh

The Battle of Khe Sanh took place in northwestern Quang Tri Province between January 21 and July 9, 1968. It started when NVA troops began bombarding the US Marine fort at Khe Sanh. The battle would become one of the longest and bloodiest, as it took 77 days until the US forces could end the siege. During the fights, Operation Niagara was launched which aimed to help the ground troops by bombing enemy positions. More than 100,000 tons of bombs were dropped over the following weeks. The estimated 20,000 NVA soldiers who hid in the surrounding hills were also fired on with 155,000 large-caliber shells.

Bombardment of the area to prepare for Operation Pegasus

After earlier operations did not succeed in freeing the surrounded fort, Operation Pegasus was launched in March. It was a combined task force of American and South Vietnamese troops to liberate the positions at Khe Sanh. They were able to free the troops, and Army staff then decided to destroy the base in order to avoid another attack. Unfortunately, the Battle of Khe Sanh distracted US intelligence from the buildup of communist forces in the south just before the Tet Offensive, which would be launched by North Vietnamese forces shortly after.

The Vietnam Disaster? From the Tet Offensive to the Kent State Shooting

34) January 31, 1968 - Tet Offensive

The Tet Offensive was probably the largest military campaign of the Vietnam War, starting on January 31, 1968, when some 70,000 North Vietnamese and Viet Cong forces attacked several cities in South Vietnam and South Vietnamese defensive positions. The name stems from the Vietnamese lunar New Year called Tet. The first wave of attacks was launched during the night hours of January 30 and aimed to prepare the main invasion the next day. Once the main operation began on January 31, attacks took place countrywide, striking more than a hundred towns and cities.

Civilians flee from the invading NVA

Once North Vietnamese soldiers had occupied a city, they would often execute hundreds if not thousands of people, as in the Massacre at Hue. The fast and devastating attacks surprised the US and South Vietnamese armies, who temporarily lost control of several cities. They then regrouped to beat back the invaders and managed to inflict massive casualties on communist soldiers. In the battle of Hue, fighting lasted for almost a month and resulted in the destruction of the city by American forces. Even though the offensive resulted in a military defeat for the NVA, it had a great effect on the US military and shocked the country. Before the Tet offensive, many did not believe the communists to be able to plan and execute such an immense military operation. Some historians argue that it marked one of the major turning points in the war, ending in American withdrawal from the region years later.

35) February 28, 1968 - Westmoreland Demands More Troops

In February 1968, General William Westmoreland met General Earle Wheeler in Saigon to discuss the future of the American involvement in Vietnam and the amount of new soldiers needed to meet their goal of defeating communism in North Vietnam. Wheeler would later write a report to President Johnson requesting 200,000 more troops in the name of Westmoreland. He stated that even though the American soldiers were better equipped and trained in every way, Viet Cong forces still operated with unbelievable freedom in the countryside. They continued to push back the South Vietnamese army and badly undermined programs for pacification in these areas. In order to successfully combat the NVA and guerilla fighters, the US forces in Vietnam would need many more soldiers.

Although his request was partially granted, Westmoreland was later replaced

The request brought Johnson in a difficult situation. A denial would mean that the US, the largest military power in the world, had no solution to a seemingly small conflict. However, if he accepted, he would have to call-up of reserves and increase war expenditures. After news of the request broke some time later, many public voices actually favored an increase in troops in Vietnam. Johnson then took the request to Congress, where it was reviewed and changed. Westmoreland's request was scaled down and an increase of only 13,500 troops was authorized. After the bill was passed, Westmoreland was brought home and replaced by General Abrams.

36) March 16, 1968 - My Lai Massacre

The My Lai Massacre was committed by US Army infantry soldiers in South Vietnam on March 16, 1968. The more than 350 victims included men, women, children, and infants. Some of the female victims were raped before being killed and mutilated. Although twenty-six soldiers were charged before a military court, only the platoon leader, Lieutenant William Calley, Jr., was convicted. He was found guilty of killing twenty-two villagers and received a life sentence, of which he only served a little more than three years.

Hugh Thompson, Jr. testified against the soldiers responsible for the Massacre

The killings, which were later called "the most gruesome episode of the Vietnam War," happened in two hamlets in the Son My village in Quang Ngai Province. They caused global outrage when news broke in November 1969. Afterwards, domestic opposition to the American involvement in Vietnam increased when the extent of the massacre and the following cover-up attempts were leaked. In the beginning, three US soldiers who had tried to stop the killings and rescue the hiding civilians were denounced as traitors by a series of US Congressmen. Only thirty years later and after several investigations were they decorated by the US Army for helping non-combatants in a war zone.

37) March 31, 1968 - President Johnson Declines Re-election

On March 31, 1968, US President Lyndon B. Johnson gave a televised speech in which he announced that he was not seeking re-election for another presidential term. His decision was largely due to decreasing public support for his decisions in the Vietnam War. The Tet Offensive had shown that any assertions about the progress of the war he or his staff gave earlier were misinformed. His credibility suffered heavily and hurt his stance as President.

President Johnson with Richard Nixon, the Republican candidate in 1968

In the months before his speech, filmed footage of battles in Vietnam regularly appeared on daily news programs watched by millions of Americans. These programs would often include scenes of carnage and showed bloody details of the war. Unlike previous wars, the news in Vietnam was not censored, and sometimes revealed shocking truths about the fighting many were not prepared to see. With increased news coverage, the American public also began to question the necessity of an American involvement. By 1968, many widespread demonstrations and unrest had erupted throughout the nation, demanding for an immediate end to the war. Along with the demonstrations, the president's criticism grew and might have had a devastating impact on the elections had Johnson candidated for another term.

38) May 10, 1969 - Battle of Hamburger Hill

The Battle of Hamburger Hill was fought by the United States and South Vietnam against NVA forces over ten days from May 10-20, 1969. Despite being of little strategic value, American commanders ordered the capture of the heavily guarded Hill 937 in the beginning of May. The battle was to be an infantry engagement, where US ground troops would take over the hill by a frontal assault. This strategy was heavily criticized, as the troops moving up the steeply sloped hill became an easy target for the well-entrenched North Vietnamese troops. Due to bad weather, NVA and guerilla forces managed to repeatedly repel American attacks and caused a great number of casualties.

US 105 mm artillery preparing the uphill invasion

Because of the grinding nature of the fighting on the hill, soldiers soon called it the "Hamburger Hill," paying tribute to a similar battle fought during the Korean War (Battle of Pork Chop Hill). In total, US casualties totaled 70 killed and 372 wounded. Although around 630 corpses were found on the hill after the battle, the actual NVA casualties remain unknown. Hamburger Hill caused a widespread discussion in the international press about unnecessary deaths of soldiers on both sides. Public outrage increased when American soldiers later abandoned the hill on June 5. The scandal directly led to the alteration of US strategy from earlier "maximum pressure" to "protective reaction," trying to lower casualties in the Vietnam War.

39) June 1969 - Nixon Advocates Vietnamization

In June 1969, the number of American troops in Vietnam peaked at 540,000. Richard Nixon, who had been elected President in 1968, then announced his plan for the "Vietnamization" of the conflict. This strategy aimed at expanding, equipping, and training the South Vietnamese forces, while assigning them a gradually increasing combat role. Nixon also promised to withdraw more than 25,000 US soldiers, once South Vietnam's army gained a higher degree of independence.

South Vietnamese unit training under American supervision

The Vietnamization strategy referred to US infantry troops specifically and did not reject air support by the US Air Force or any kind of passive military aid. It consisted of two important components: The first step was to strengthen the South Vietnamese armed force in numbers, leadership, and equipment, while the second step was to extend the pacification program in the region. During the next months, promising candidates of the South Vietnamese army were enrolled in American military academies, allowing them to lead infantry operations in the future. The policy fit well into the broader goals of the Nixon administration, where the United States would no longer aim to contain communism in small countries, but seek peaceful resolutions by cooperating with bigger world powers, mainly the Soviet Union. Nixon's chief advisor, Henry Kissinger, was ordered to negotiate diplomatic policies with Soviet statesman Anatoly Dobrynin and open high-level contact with China.

40) September 2, 1969 - Ho Chi Minh Dies

On September 2, 1969, six years before his army seized Saigon, the North Vietnamese president died. His death was announced to the public one day after a heart attack caused him to be hospitalized. Having been the sole leader of the communist movement in the country, many North Vietnamese reacted shocked to the news. Even though Minh had already stepped down from power in 1965, he remained an inspiration and popular figurehead and for almost all Vietnamese people fighting for his cause. In his honor, Saigon, the former capital of South Vietnam, would be renamed Ho Chi Minh City after the war.

Minh around 1946

Born as Nguyen Sinh, Con he later changed his name to Ho Chi Minh ("Ho, the Bringer of Light"), after Japan invaded Vietnam at the beginning of the Second World War From 1941 onward, he became a vital part of the Viet Minh independence movement and in 1945 established the Democratic Republic of Vietnam under a communist government. His army defeated the French Union at the battle of Dien Bien Phu in 1954, which led to the Geneva Accords dividing Vietnam into North and South Vietnam. During the next years, Ho Chi Minh committed his efforts to building a communist society in North Vietnam. As this meant complete independence from European or American colonialism, new war broke out in the South when communist-led guerrillas attacked the US supported regime in Saigon. Early efforts for a diplomatic resolution of the conflict failed, and soon Minh directed his forces in an all-out war against the US military. As the highest leader of the communist north, he provided inspirational guidance to his people, which became increasingly important after his health deteriorated and day-by-day policies were taken over by others. Minh remained the embodiment of the revolution even after his death, and is a communist icon until today.

41) December 15, 1970 - Nixon Declares War Is Ending

As the US military implemented Nixon's policy of Vietnamization, he told the press on December 15, 1970, that "the war would soon be ending." He predicted that the South Vietnamese forces would soon be able to successfully defend their positions against the NVA and Viet Cong without American help, as US military experts trained South Vietnamese forces in tactics and combat. In his address, the president pointed out that some 60,000 US troops were already ordered to withdraw from Vietnam and that the 25th Infantry Division was leaving the country that same day. Nixon also believed that the continuing military aid would equip South Vietnam with more modern weapons, which would significantly increase their military strength.

Nixon explaining the Cambodian incursion, which would follow only a few months after his initial address

Most of Nixon's predictions later proved false. Only a few months after the address, he ordered US and South Vietnamese soldiers to invade Cambodia as part of the Cambodia Campaign, which led to national protests and the Kent State shooting. Even though troop numbers were decreased during the next years, fighting continued with no victory in sight. Unlike Nixon believed, the military aid did not do much against the NVA, which actually increased its pressure on South Vietnamese positions. In 1972, the North Vietnamese would launch the Easter Campaign, a massive invasion of South

Vietnam, which was only brought to a halt with the help of US airpower. As it turned out, the war was far from over.

42) April 30, 1970 - Cambodia Campaign Begins

On April 30, 1970, President Nixon held a televised speech to the nation, explaining the need to cut off North Vietnamese supplies by attacking Cambodia. His address was a direct response to the growing North Vietnamese aggression on American positions. The Cambodian Campaign was to become a series of military operations executed in eastern Cambodia during mid-1970 by American and South Vietnamese forces. The goal of the campaign was to defeat the approximately 45,000 North Vietnamese troops in the eastern border regions of Cambodia. The country's military weakness and official neutrality were used by the NVA as a safe zone where communist forces could be stationed and supplies brought into the country. As Nixon advanced with his policy of Vietnamization and withdrawal, border threats such as this needed to be eliminated to guarantee the South Vietnamese government's security in the future.

South Vietnamese tanks invading Cambodia

In total, thirteen major operations were launched by South Vietnamese Army in Vietnam between April 29 and July 22 and by American forces between May 1 and June 30. The operations were supported by a change in the Cambodian government when Prince Norodom Sihanouk was replaced by pro-US General Lon Nol. This led to an initial boost in confidence as many supply routes were cut off and enemy equipment captured. However, the military campaign failed to capture North Vietnamese positions or eliminate communist troops, which is why it is difficult to call the invasion a success.

43) May 4, 1970 - Kent State Shootings

On May 1, 1973, students at Kent State University in Ohio organized a massive public demonstration against the US invasion of Cambodia. The demonstration quickly grew in size, and on the second day, a series of students torched the R.O.T.C. building on the Kent university campus. The same day, the mayor of Kent called in the National Guard to bring the situation under control. Over the next days, attempts to disperse the growing crowd failed, and on the fourth day of the protests, chaos ensued when several groups of demonstrators refused to follow orders given by the National Guard. In response, members of the Guard shot into the crowd, killing four and wounding nine, leaving one of them paralyzed for life. The four victims included two protesters and two students walking to class.

News of the so-called "Kent State massacre" spread throughout the country and college campuses all across the country shut down in protest. Some four million students went on strike while the press and media criticized the actions of the National Guard. Images of the dead and injured at Kent State were released in newspapers, gaining worldwide attention and amplifying sentiments against the US invasion of Cambodia. One photograph showing student John Filo on the ground after being shot won a Pulitzer Prize and became the most enduring images of the shootings and later of the protests against the Vietnam War.

James Weber

The Last Years: From Operation Linebacker to the Fall of Saigon

44) May 9, 1972 - Operation Linebacker

Operation Linebacker was launched in response to the NVA's Easter Offensive, a massive invasion into South Vietnam designed to win vast lands of territory. The Easter Offensive began on March 30, after negotiations between the US and North Vietnam at the Paris Peace Accords failed. It struck on three fronts simultaneously, catching much of the American and South Vietnamese troops defending the area off guard and causing heavy casualties. The following week, US military began Operation Linebacker to slow down the transportation of supplies and equipment for Easter Offensive and therefore give ground troops the necessary time to regroup.

American bomber destroying the Hải Dương Bridge

The operation's aerial bombardment had several objectives: Destroying railroad bridges and isolating North Vietnam from its outside sources of supply, as well as targeting transshipment and storage points, while eliminating North Vietnam's air defense system. At the same time, a naval operation called Pocket Money would block North Vietnam's imports by sea. The US administration believed that together, Operation Linebacker and Pocket Money would cripple the NVA's lines of communication and supply, forcing the government to give up the Easter Offensive. Their plan worked, and the offensive stalled, convincing Hanoi to return to the bargaining table by early August. Nixon then ordered a stop to all bombing on October 23.

45) January 27, 1973 - Paris Peace Accords Signed

The Paris Peace Accords of 1973 were a direct result of the North Vietnamese Easter Offensive and the American Operation Linebacker. Earlier negotiations already took place in the 60s, but were delayed several times, often over years. The bombardment during Operation Linebacker forced North Vietnam's government to re-initiate peace talks in 1972 involving negotiations about an end to the US involvement in Vietnam. An agreement was signed on January 27, 1973, by representatives of all three countries, though it was not ratified by the United States Senate.

The signing of the peace accords in Paris

The main negotiators of the Peace Accords were Henry Kissinger (United States National Security Advisor) and Le Duc Tho (Vietnamese politburo member). Both were later awarded with the Nobel Peace Prize, but Le Duc Tho refused to accept it. Unfortunately, the agreement had little practical effect on the war, and was routinely flouted by the Saigon and the Hanoi government. North Vietnam also continued to build up its military infrastructure in the controlled areas, and two years later launched the successful invasion that ended South Vietnam's status as an independent country.

46) March 29, 1973 - US Withdraws Troops from Vietnam

As part of the peace accords, the US agreed to withdraw all of its combat troops from South Vietnam, the last of which left the

Vietnam War In 50 Events

country on March 29, 1973. In the meantime, North Vietnam released the remaining American prisoners of war. This marked the end of an eight-year intervention in Vietnam with approximately 58,000 Americans dead. However, even after the withdrawal, some 7,000 Americans, mostly civilian employees of the Department of Defense stayed in Saigon and the surrounding regions. They were part of Nixon's Vietnamization, which aimed to support South Vietnam in defending its positions against North Vietnam in the months to follow. Despite peace had been officially declared, many were convinced the war between the North and the South would go on.

Released prisoners of war on a plane to the US

Unfortunately, their predictions turned out to be true. Just before the last US troops departed, the North violated several agreements of the peace accords, including the cease-fire. A few months later full-scale war had resumed – this time without US support. By the end of the next year (1974), the South Vietnamese government reported that more than 70,000 of their soldiers and civilians had been killed in. The communists would continue their invasion until 1975 when they took Saigon and South Vietnam surrendered. In total, as many as two million Vietnamese civilians and soldiers were killed during the war.

47) June 1973 - Case–Church Amendment

In early 1973, North Vietnam violated the ceasefire and invaded the south. In June, despite renewed fighting, the US Congress voted to prohibit any further US combat role in Vietnam. This legislation, called the Case–Church Amendment (named after its principal sponsors Senator Clifford P. Case and Senator Frank Church), prohibited not only involvement in Vietnam, but also in Laos and Cambodia, unless the president could secure Congressional approval in advance. The legislation had already been proposed in August 1972 but was defeated 48 - 42 in the US Senate.

Senator Clifford P. Case, one of the most popular supports of the amendment

After the 1972 election proponents of the law reintroduced it, this time successfully, being roved by the Senate Foreign Relations Committee on May 13. After it became apparent that the law would pass, Secretary of State Henry Kissinger and President Richard Nixon lobbied heavily to have the deadline extended in order to provide further help to South Vietnam. The amendment passed the United States Congress in June by a margin of 325 - 86 in the House, and later by 73 - 16 in the Senate, both times exceeding the required two-thirds majority to override a presidential veto. With the amendment passed, any US support in Vietnam, such as bombing, would have to end on August 15, 1973.

48) August 9, 1974 - President Nixon Resigns

On August 9, 1974, President Richard M. Nixon became the first US in American history to resign. His decision, which he announced in a televised address to the nation, was largely based on impeachment proceedings against him for his involvement in the Watergate scandal and the lost support by both the public and Congress after the Vietnam War. He then resigned as the 37th president and left in a helicopter from the White House to his family estate in California. Nixon was succeeded by Vice President Gerald R. Ford, who later pardoned him from any crimes he may have committed while being president.

Demonstrators demanding Nixon's impeachment

Leading up to his resignation, five men were arrested in 1972 for wiretapping the Democratic National Committee headquarters in Washington, D.C. Although the Nixon administration initially denied any involvement, reporters later discovered evidence proving otherwise. The Watergate affair soon escalated with publicly televised proceedings and new accusations breaking daily. Evidence of political espionage was uncovered in which Nixon and the re-election committee appeared to be directly involved. In July 1974, three articles of impeachment were adopted against President Nixon. With public confidence in the president decreasing, it seemed a change in office was inevitable. Several days later, Nixon announced his resignation.

49) April 9, 1975 - Battle of Xuan Loc

The Battle of Xuan Loc was one of the last major battles of the Vietnam War. South Vietnam committed almost all its remaining troops, especially the 18th Infantry Division under General Le Minh Dao to defend the town of Xuan Loc. The battle was fought between April 9 and 21, 1975, when Xuan Loc was captured by the North Vietnamese 4th Army Corps. The fall of Xuan Loc also meant the fall of the last defensive line of country's capital, Saigon.

Picture of South Vietnamese soldiers celebrating the initial defense of the city

After the last US troops left the country, North Vietnam's military forces invaded the northern provinces of South Vietnam virtually unopposed. As defensive positions were overrun, many South

Vietnamese units simply dissolved without putting up any sort of resistance. The heavy defeats suffered by the troops prompted the country's National Assembly to doubt President Nguyen Van Thieu's handling of the war and placed him under great pressure to resign. In order to save South Vietnam, the president then ordered his last military units, known as "The Super Men," to defend Xuan Loc at all cost. The soldiers managed to fight off early attempts by the NVA to capture the town, forcing the North Vietnamese government to change its battle plan. Implementing a new strategy and with the help of new forces, the NVA then successfully invaded the city taking the remaining South Vietnamese soldiers as prisoners.

50) April 30, 1975 - The Fall of Saigon

After the NVA crushed the South Vietnamese last stand at the Battle of Xuan Loc, there were no relevant defensive positions between the North Vietnamese army and Saigon left. When NVA tanks rolled into the city on April 30, 1975, it marked the end of the Vietnam War and the beginning of a transition period leading to the formal reunification of the country into a socialist republic, under the Communist Party of Vietnam.

Operation Frequent Wind saved thousands of civilians from the incoming NVA troops

NVA forces, led by General Van Tien Dung, started their final attack on Saigon on April 29. The city was hit by heavy artillery bombardment, which killed the last two US servicemen to die in the war. In the afternoon of the next day, the troops had taken hold of the most important points of the city and flew the North Vietnamese flag over the presidential palace. The South Vietnamese government surrendered a few hours later. Before the city was captured, almost all the American military personnel and civilians in Saigon were evacuated. The operation called Frequent Wind consisted of the largest helicopter evacuation in history, as more than 6,500 people were evacuated from various points in Saigon by helicopter. After its fall, the city was renamed Ho Chi Minh city, although the name was rarely used outside of official business. Everyday life was slowly restored, despite many businesses and the US embassy having been looted. Later, General Tran Van Tra was put in charge of the city and held a victory rally on May 7.

Other Books in the *History in 50 Events* Series

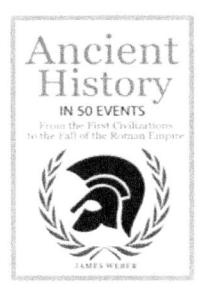

Printed in Great Britain
by Amazon